Greeting the Morning

MAYA ANGELOU

by Sarah E. King

A Gateway Biography
The Millbrook Press
Brookfield, Connecticut

Cover photo courtesy of Chick Harrity/U.S. News & World Report
Background cover photo courtesy of Superstock

Photos courtesy of Mary Ellen Mark/Library: pp. 4, 28, 39 (bottom);
Arkansas History Commission: p. 8; Bettmann Archive: pp. 10, 11; Art
Resource, New York: p. 13 (top); The Schomburg Center for Research
in Black Culture, New York Public Library: pp. 13 (bottom), 19; State
Historical Society of Missouri, Columbia: p. 16; UPI/Bettmann: pp. 21,
25, 30; Wide World Photos: pp. 33, 37; W. L. DeDecker/Gamma Lia-
ison: p. 39 (top); Chick Harrity/U.S. News & World Report: p. 42.

Library of Congress Cataloging-in-Publication Data
King, Sarah E., 1957–
Maya Angelou : greeting the morning / by Sarah E. King.
p.   cm.—(A Gateway biography)
Includes bibliographical references and index.
Summary: Examines the life of the African-American poet, from her
childhood in the segregated South to her rise to prominence as a
writer.
ISBN 1-56294-431-2 (lib. bdg.) ISBN 1-56294-725-7 (pbk.)
1. Angelou, Maya—Biography—Juvenile literature.   2. Afro-
American women authors—20th century—Biography—Juvenile
literature.   [1. Angelou, Maya.   2. Authors, American.   3. Afro-
Americans—Biography.]   I. Title.   II. Series.
PS3551.N464Z74   1994
818'.5409—dc20   [B]   93-4572   CIP   AC

Published by The Millbrook Press
2 Old New Milford Road
Brookfield, Connecticut 06804

Maya Angelou

Maya Angelou (left) with her mother. The two were separated and reunited several times.

Maya Angelou was three years old when she went to live with her grandmother in Stamps, Arkansas. She and her brother, Bailey, had been living with their parents in California. The family had moved west from St. Louis, Missouri, where Maya was born in 1928.

But times were hard, and Maya and Bailey's parents decided that it was best to separate. The children's mother, Vivian Baxter Johnson, felt that she could not properly care for the young ones on her own. So she carefully placed name tags around the wrists of her two small children and pinned their tickets inside her son's jacket pocket for safekeeping. Then she placed the tiny pair on a train headed east.

The name on Maya's tag read "Marguerite Johnson," for that was the name she was given at birth. But all her life, she would be known as "Maya." It was Bailey's special nickname for her, short for "my sister." Even later, when she took her husband's last name, she kept her brother's nickname for her. She became known as Maya Angelou, one of America's most famous writers.

Maya and Bailey learned to look out for one another on the long train ride across the country. The strong brother-sister bond that grew up between them had its roots in that early trip. Maya was too young to remember much else about those long hours spent together. But she always recalled how kind the other passengers had been. As the train neared Arkansas, they even shared the fried chicken and potato salad from their own lunch boxes with the frightened children. This was the children's first taste of black Southern hospitality. Perhaps this moving picnic helped to make the trip seem more like an adventure to the little girl, and less like a scary journey to a strange, new place to live among unknown people.

Maya and Bailey arrived safely in the small town of Stamps and began their new life with "Momma," as they called their father's mother. The children never knew their grandfather Johnson. Their grandmother remarried a man named Henderson. But he no longer lived with her when they arrived.

Momma Henderson lived with their Uncle Willie in the rear of the general store that she had owned for twenty-five years. Everyone in town knew and respected Annie Henderson as a good businesswoman and as a church-going member of the community. More than just a place to buy groceries, The Store, as it was simply called, was a gathering spot for the black folk of Stamps. On hot summer days, the local barbers offered their customers haircuts and shoeshines in the shade of the front porch. There was gossip and laughter and cool lemonade at Momma's Store.

Sometimes Maya and her brother helped out behind the counter at The Store. They learned how to measure out the right amounts of flour and sugar and to make change for the customers. Once in a while they couldn't resist treating themselves to one of the fat pickles from the big barrels that lined the walls of the shop. They could only gaze longingly at cans of sweet, juicy pineapple rings Momma kept stashed high up on shelves. Such treats were served only on holidays and special occasions.

Because of a childhood accident, Uncle Willie could not get about easily. Most of the time, he sat

An Arkansas storefront of the 1930s. People could buy food, clothes, tools, and almost anything else at stores like this and Momma Henderson's. Such places were also town meeting centers.

perched on a stool in The Store. His seat was placed to catch the cool breeze in the summer and the warmth of the pot-bellied stove in winter. From there, Uncle Willie kept a sharp eye on his niece and nephew, the customers, and the comings and goings on the street.

It was the early 1930s, and Stamps was in the heart of the segregated South. Segregation meant that black people and white people lived separately. Folks called it the Jim Crow South, named after the laws that divided the races. The black side of Stamps, called the Negro section, was the poorer side of town. Here Maya and Bailey lived with their grandmother and uncle.

Maya could look out the window of her grandmother's Store and see the cotton field across the street. Many of her grandmother's friends and customers just barely made a living by picking cotton, piece by piece, plant after plant, row upon row. They worked until they had filled enough bags to trade for food and clothing money. It was backbreaking work, and Momma said prayers of thanks every night that she and her grandchildren were spared that hard life.

Above: Even when it came to getting a drink of water, Jim Crow laws forced blacks and whites apart. This 1939 photo shows a segregated water fountain in Oklahoma. Facing page: This photo shows Mississippi cotton pickers trailing long white sacks. Like the workers Maya saw, they had to fill such sacks many times to earn a living.

Maya, like her older brother, was good at school. They both could say their times tables lickety-split, faster than any of the other children. Maya also loved to read. On her list of favorite writers were William Shakespeare and Edgar Allan Poe. But she had a special spot in her heart for the African-American poets Paul Laurence Dunbar and Langston Hughes. How could she ever have imagined, all those years ago, that one day she would be named by little girls and boys on their own lists of favorite writers!

In addition to school, Maya and Bailey had daily chores. Besides working in The Store, they also learned to feed the pigs their mushy mixture of corn and sour mash. Maya's tall, strong, hardworking grandmother believed in routines for her family. There were regular, icy-cold washups watched over by Momma, who insisted on cleanliness. And, of course, there were weekly trips to church, for Maya's grandmother was a God-fearing woman.

Just keeping this family together, with food on the table and clean, sewn and resewn clothing, was a remarkable feat during those years. When money

There was no
segregation in
Maya's choice
of authors. She
loved the work
of both William
Shakespeare (left)
and Paul Laurence
Dunbar (below).

13

ran out one winter, Momma began trading goods directly from her store to get the things they needed. Little Maya made a sign with crayons telling what each item was worth in trade.

One day, a big man with a smile to match pulled up in a gray car outside of Momma's Store. This tall stranger with the hearty laugh turned out to be Maya and Bailey's father. He had come all the way from California. Except for yearly Christmas presents, the children had rarely heard from their parents. Sometimes, Maya had even imagined that they were dead.

Papa Bailey Johnson's visit caused quite a stir. Maya and Bailey soon learned that he had come to take them away with him. Maya was sad to be leaving Momma, but she was also excited about the trip ahead. Both children were eager to see their mother once again.

After a long drive by car, Maya and Bailey were reunited with their mother in St. Louis, Missouri. As Maya described it years later, it was "love at first sight" for the two children. She remembered meeting a very pretty woman, more like a stranger than a mother. She also remembered how quickly they warmed to each other. The children said good-bye once more to their father. And so began their new life with the woman they called "Mother Dear" and their Grandmother Baxter.

St. Louis was very different from Stamps. The streets, for all their pavement, seemed dirtier. The buildings were all larger. There were new foods to try, like the delicious thin-sliced ham from the deli. And there were other changes to get used to. The school Maya and Bailey now attended was very different from the one they had known back in Stamps. After the familiar slow drawl of the South, people seemed to be talking a different language. And nothing in Stamps had prepared them for this city full of buses and trucks and people who always seemed to be in a hurry.

While she was living in St. Louis, a terrible thing happened to Maya. When she was eight years old, she was sexually abused by a man friend of her mother's. One day, while they were in the house alone, the man touched Maya in ways he had never done when her mother was present. At first Maya

A busy section of St. Louis, Missouri, in 1929, several years before Maya and Bailey lived there. In 1927, pilot Charles A. Lindbergh made a historic flight from the United States to France in a plane called (after the city) the Spirit of St. Louis.

told no one, but her mother and Bailey noticed how upset she was and she told them the truth. They took her to the hospital to be examined and helped her by listening and talking to her.

Although what had happened was not her fault, Maya felt so guilty when she had to testify against the man in court that she decided after the trial not to talk at all. Her mother and her brother understood Maya's pain, but the rest of the family grew impatient with Maya's silence. Maya's mother thought that it would be best for her daughter to be away from the place where something so horrible had happened. So it was decided that the brother and sister would return to their grandmother in Arkansas. This was not meant to be a punishment. But Maya blamed herself for having been sent away. It was only many years later that she realized that she had done nothing wrong.

A*fter St. Louis,* Stamps at first seemed like a tiny and drab place. Still, for a time, Maya and Bailey were the center of attention. Friends and neighbors stopped by constantly to hear their stories about the big city "up North." Of course, Bailey always did all the talking. It would be a whole year before Maya began to talk again.

The person who helped her to understand that it was safe to trust adults again was a neighbor and friend of her grandmother. Her name was Bertha Flowers, and she was known as the richest African-American woman in Stamps. Maya had always watched the educated and elegantly dressed Mrs. Flowers as she passed by Momma's Store. Often, Mrs. Flowers would stop to chat with Maya's grandmother, and she always had a kind word for the quiet little girl.

Maya was surprised and delighted when one day Mrs. Flowers asked Maya to join her. Together they walked to Mrs. Flower's tidy home. Once there, Maya was invited to share homemade cookies and lemonade while Mrs. Flowers read aloud to her. As if in a dream, Maya listened to this woman's beautiful voice. Mrs. Flowers then offered to lend Maya books to read whenever she liked. But Maya had to promise to read them aloud, to learn to be proud of the sound of her own voice. So impressed was Maya by the generosity of her new friend that

A black church in Little Rock, Arkansas, in 1935. For Maya, as for many black Southerners, going to church meant more than attending religious services. It also meant celebrating the black community during a time of discrimination.

she forgot to mistrust adults and began speaking again.

As time passed, life in Stamps took on its old familiarity, and Maya and Bailey once more felt at home there. On certain Sundays they would go with their grandmother to revival meetings. These were packed, noisy gatherings in the name of the Lord, held inside huge tents pitched for the occasion. It seemed as if all of black Stamps turned out for these events. There was much preaching and saving of souls. To finish up, the rich earthy tones of gospel music rose up toward the heavens.

On other days, there were town-wide picnics to attend and movies to save up for. And Maya never forgot one special night when the whole town gathered around the radio in Momma's Store to listen to a boxing match. This was no ordinary sporting event. This was the African-American boxer Joe Louis, the Brown Bomber, defending his heavyweight title. It seemed to Maya that the whole world was leaning forward to better hear the announcer that evening. No one even dared to breathe as they listened closely for the outcome of the match between Louis and his German oppo-

The triumphs of sports figures like Joe Louis were also causes for celebration for blacks. Here Louis stands over his defeated opponent, Max Schmeling.

nent. And no one could contain their pride when Joe Louis was declared the winner. It meant quite a lot to the humble black folk of Stamps that someone who once had also been as poor as they were, who had also suffered the indignity of unfair Jim Crow laws, was known as the world champion. Maya joined happily in the celebration.

As she slowly became a young woman, Maya learned many things about growing up. She learned how to make and treasure friends when she met Louise Kendricks, a schoolmate who shared her love of books. She also had her first crush when a boy in her school sent her a valentine.

There were more bitter lessons in those years as well. Maya was growing up in a time when racism still dictated that African Americans should look forward to becoming maids or athletes, instead of writers or scientists. Once, when she was suffering from a toothache, she learned that a white dentist could refuse to treat her, even if no black dentist could be found for miles around. But instead of defeating the young girl, these injustices made her more determined than ever to make something of herself. All her life, she had seen her grandmother face hard times without giving up hope.

As Maya and Bailey began to grow up, Momma realized that she wasn't getting any younger. It was time, she decided, for them to try living with their mother once again. By then, Vivian Baxter had divorced and moved back to California. Because the train fare to such a faraway place was high, they would have to make separate trips. As Momma was able to scrape together the funds to pay for each ticket, first she and Maya, and later Bailey, made the long journey.

It was the first time in their lives that Maya and Bailey were separated. This, and the thought of being reunited with their beautiful but unfamiliar mother, made Maya nervous. This time, she was unable to enjoy the sights and sounds of the trip back across the country as she had as a tot. Once the small family was reunited in California, it was time to say good-bye to Momma. She headed back to Arkansas to be with Uncle Willie.

Just as Maya and Bailey were settling into their

new lives in California, World War II began. Thirteen-year-old Maya was now witness to a form of racism different from what she had seen in the South. This time, it was Japanese Americans who were treated unfairly because America was at war with Japan. Many Asian-American families were forced to sell or leave their homes and businesses and go to live in crowded camps because of their background. It was as unjust as the Jim Crow laws of the Deep South, but few people spoke out. Later, when she became a well-known writer, Maya would.

Maya, who had always been a good student, was given a scholarship to attend the California Labor School when she was fourteen years old. She also took evening classes in drama and dance.

At sixteen, a year older than Maya, Bailey was the first to leave home. He decided to learn the railroad business, and so he took a job with the Southern Pacific railroad company. Maya sadly said good-bye to her brother. For so many years he had been her closest companion.

Bailey's leaving left a hole in Maya's life, and she decided that it was time to take a job herself.

A food line at a camp, or "relocation center," in Denver, Colorado. Thousands of Japanese Americans were held at such camps during World War II.

Maya looked around and decided that she would like to become a conductorette on the San Francisco streetcars. She would wear a crisp navy blue uniform and collect the passengers' money as they got on the trolley. She would be just like the neatly dressed young women with important-looking change holders hanging from their belts that she saw on her daily rides. But when she went to apply for the job, she was told that she couldn't even fill out an application form. African Americans, male or female, still were not allowed to serve as conductors or conductorettes.

Maya refused to accept this unfair practice. Day after day, she went back to the place where the hiring was done. Finally, one day she was allowed to fill out the forms for the job. After a number of tests, she was hired. Maya became the first African-American conductorette on the San Francisco streetcar.

For a while, the excitement of becoming a working girl turned Maya's interest away from school. But she had always trusted her brother Bailey's advice, and now he urged her to get her high school diploma. The war had finally ended, and days for celebrating the victories over Germany and Japan were declared. The year was 1945. When Mission High School in San Francisco held its graduation ceremonies, Maya was among the students receiving their diplomas. As the nation celebrated the end of the war, it was also a day of personal victory for the little girl from Stamps who had always loved books.

Shortly after her graduation, Maya went to her mother with some news that she could no longer keep secret. In a few months she was due to give birth to a baby. Because she and the baby's father did not love one another, they decided not to get married. A few months later her son was born. Maya named the child Clyde Bailey Johnson. She could not help feeling a bit scared when she thought of all that she had to learn about being a mother. But she also felt a tremendous amount of love when she looked at her sleeping child. At the age of seventeen she had become a single mother.

Vivian Baxter, now a grandmother, stood by her daughter. Still, Maya felt that it was time for

Maya gazing at a photo of baby Clyde.

her to make a life of her own. She needed to find a way to support herself and her child. She tried many jobs in those first years of motherhood. For a while she became a cook in a restaurant, serving up steaming dishes of the Southern-style cooking of her girlhood. She also tried her hand at waitressing and driving a car. In lean times, she took two jobs to keep food on the table for her and little Guy, as her son came to be known. But always, Maya kept her mind alive by continuing to read. When she could, she took dance lessons as well.

No doubt her love of music drew Maya to take a job in a local record store. She was happy to be working steadily. She also enjoyed helping the customers to find their selections from among the recordings by the great jazz musicians of the time such as Charlie Parker, Dizzy Gillespie, and Thelonius Monk.

While working in the record store, Maya met Tosh Angelos. He was a Greek sailor who shared her love of African-American music and her affection for Guy. Before long, Maya and Tosh were married. The new Mrs. Angelos quit her job, and for a time was happy staying at home and being a

Saxophonist Charlie Parker. One of the greatest American musicians of all time, Parker made music that rose above racial divisions. Whites as well as blacks like Maya loved his work.

wife and mother. But Maya had always been active and independent. As time wore on, she became less and less happy with her role as a housewife. Maya began to miss her old life-style and her freedom. Finally, Maya and Tosh decided to divorce. Once again, Maya was on her own. She began looking for a new way to support herself and her son.

Music and the arts had always been a part of Maya's life. Gospel spirituals had filled the church every Sunday back in Stamps. The soulful words and rhythms of those songs were like second nature to her. Meanwhile, the lessons she had invested in all those years had turned her into a graceful dancer. Maya was ready to give the difficult entertainment business a try.

Despite her years of training and natural talent, it was rough going at first. It was a life of late hours, shabby nightclubs, and poor pay. Still, Maya was learning "the business." During this period she first adopted the stage name that she would keep throughout her life. Because there was another performer named Marguerite in the club where she danced, she had decided to go by "Maya." When it was suggested that her last name, Johnson, was too common for "show biz," she invented an easier-to-say version of her married name. Somehow, the new combination—Maya Angelou—seemed to fit her just right.

Maya now began to work hard to learn her new craft. It was the early 1950s, and there were not many good roles in show business for African-Americans. The powerful men who decided who got jobs thought that most people didn't want to see black performers. But Maya was patient and persistent. At last, she was rewarded for her hard work. She was chosen to be a member of the all-black cast for the musical *Porgy and Bess.* The show was about to tour Europe, and Maya could hardly contain her excitement over this chance to travel to places like Paris and Rome. Guy, now a toddler, would stay with his grandmother in San Francisco.

In Europe the company was a success wherever it performed. Maya saw many exciting places, and the cast was like a second family. But after a while she began to miss her son a great deal and

Another example of how the arts crossed color boundaries was Porgy and Bess, *the musical in which Maya won a part. Although written by a white composer, George Gershwin, it drew on black experience. A scene from a 1935 production appears here.*

knew it was time to return to the States. She did not want Guy to grow up without a mother.

Back home again, Maya made a living as a nightclub singer. It wasn't as glamorous as touring with a production company, but it allowed her to be near her son and mother. It also gave her some time to grow as a person. For Maya it was a time for observing the world around her. She noted tiny details wherever she went. Later, she put into words what she saw and felt at that time. It was the beginning of her career as a writer.

Maya approached this new phase of her life with all the energy she had brought to other challenges. In the late 1950s and early 1960s, there was only one place for a black writer to be: New York City. Many of the best writers of the day were already living there. Maya packed up her little family for the move back east. In New York, Maya became a member of the Harlem Writers Guild. Every week, a group of African-American men and women got together to read and listen to each other's writing. They were friends, but they were honest and open when they commented on what they heard. Maya listened and learned.

But her life in New York was not devoted only to writing. It was the time of the civil rights movement in America. Black people across the nation, headed by leaders like Dr. Martin Luther King, Jr., were demanding their equal rights under the law. Maya joined the struggle and soon became known as an activist for racial justice. At Dr. King's invitation, she became the Northern coordinator of the Southern Christian Leadership Conference. She organized meetings and joined in marches aimed at changing unfair laws.

It was a great moment in her life when she first met Reverend King and heard him speak. His rich voice and stirring message of brotherhood and sisterhood left quite an impression on his audience, including Maya. So inspired were the members of her group that night that they decided to put on a show. The performance would raise money for the cause of desegregation in the South and fairer laws for everyone. Maya helped write the show's script, which was called *Cabaret for Freedom.*

Through her work as a writer, a civil rights activist, and an entertainer, Maya began to meet many of the best-known black men and women of her day. She was proud to be introduced to entertainers like the famed jazz singer Billie Holiday, actors like Harry Belafonte and Godfrey Cambridge, the singer Abbe Lane, and the Muslim activist Malcolm X. Maya moved in these new circles with the same proud grace she brought to all of her activities.

At the same time, Maya was becoming famous in her own right. In 1969 she published the first and best known of the books about her life, *I Know Why the Caged Bird Sings.* This book, which told the story of her childhood in Stamps, was so successful that she was asked to make it into a script for television.

Maya also wrote many books of poetry. Her poems talked about being a young woman, about learning to love, and about the struggle for black pride. In one poem, "Harlem Hopscotch," she wrote of how being a winner isn't always about who gets the most points in a game: "Both feet flat, the game is done. / They think I lost. I think I won." The rules of hopscotch say that you lose if you stop hopping on one foot. But to Maya Angelou just standing upright, with both feet on the ground,

Maya holding a copy of the book that made her famous, I Know Why the Caged Bird Sings.

is also a challenge. Her poetry offered a message of hope.

In the early 1960s, Maya met and fell in love with an African freedom fighter named Vusumzi Make. His struggle against *apartheid,* the South African government's rule that separated the races, became hers. For a time during the 1970s, she moved with Guy to Africa to be with and support Make. As Americans, she and Guy were stunned to see an entire continent of people their own color. The joy they felt at seeing the brightly colored goods of the marketplaces and feeling the hot African sun on their dark skin reminded them that their ancestors had come from this land. In a sense, they felt as if they were coming home.

Although Maya and her son enjoyed many aspects of their lives in Africa, there were problems as well. Maya's life had become a hectic mix of work, writing, and politics. And once again, she found herself trying to fit the mold of being a good mate and mother. Only now this meant holding a job, cooking lavish meals, and keeping a clean

Black South Africans march in protest of apartheid as whites look on. Maya and many other Americans joined the fight against the country's racial division.

Although Maya left Africa, she carried her experience home with her. In this photo she stands next to her collection of African art.

house. Eventually, she felt the need to leave Africa and to return with Guy to the life she knew best.

All her life, Maya Angelou had been a proud, independent Southern woman. In 1981 she was offered a lifetime position as a professor at Wake Forest University in Winston-Salem, North Carolina. She welcomed the chance to return to the slower pace of the South she knew so well and to teach others about the literature she had always loved.

This did not mean that Maya Angelou's life was without excitement. She continued to travel and speak to young audiences about the lessons she had learned throughout her life and about her writing. She received honors and awards wherever she went. Many people now think of Maya Angelou as a living symbol of African-American culture and as a role model for young writers of all races.

When President Bill Clinton was planning his inauguration celebration in January 1993, he wanted someone to write a special poem to honor the occasion. He chose Maya Angelou for the job. Like the new president, Maya was raised in a small town in Arkansas. And, like him, she had come from a poor childhood and, through hard work, had become the best at what she did. She had become an example of the American Dream.

Once again, Maya was faced with a new challenge. When she accepted the president's invitation, she knew what kind of poem she wanted to write. It should be a poem that represented all the different kinds of people who made up the United States. A poem that spoke to and for everybody. She wanted to remind us all of past hardships overcome and also to point the way to future hope.

On a clear, cold January morning, before the entire nation, Maya Angelou stepped up to the microphone and delivered her poem. She had titled it "On the Pulse of Morning." At that moment, people throughout the world saw how a little girl from the American South who once refused to speak could become a great and respected spokeswoman for an entire country. It was as if she were telling the world that we all have something worth saying. Once more, Maya Angelou was reminding us why the caged bird sings.

Throughout her life, Maya Angelou experienced separations from personal changes and from racism. In her poem "On the Pulse of Morning," written for the 1993 inauguration, she spoke of bringing people together. President Bill Clinton (right) and the nation greeted her message.

In her poem "On the Pulse of Morning," Maya Angelou speaks for people of all different races, backgrounds, and ages—male and female, rich and poor. Her message is one of remembering where, as a nation, Americans have been, including some dark moments like slavery and segregation. But it is especially a poem about the hope that comes from facing each morning squarely and greeting it with joy:

. . . Lift up your faces,
      you have a piercing need
For this bright morning dawning for you.
History, despite its wrenching pain,
Cannot be unlived, but if faced
With courage, need not be lived again. . . .

Here, on the pulse of this new day
You may have the grace to look up and out
And into your sister's eyes, and into
Your brother's face, your country
And say simply
With hope—
Good morning.

Chronology

1928 Born Marguerite Annie Johnson on April 4 in St. Louis, Missouri.

1931 Sent with brother Bailey to live in Stamps, Arkansas, with grandmother.

1940 Graduates with top honors from Lafayette County Training school.

1945 Receives high school diploma; Clyde (Guy) Bailey Johnson is born.

1954–55 Tours Europe with the cast of *Porgy and Bess.*

1959 Moves to New York; joins the Harlem Writers Guild.

1969 *I Know Why the Caged Bird Sings* is published.

1971 Adapts *Caged Bird* for television; plays Kunte Kinte's grandmother in the television miniseries *Roots.*

1975 Named Woman of the Year by the *Ladies' Home Journal.*

1981 Accepts lifetime position as a literature professor at Wake Forest University in Winston-Salem, North Carolina.

1993 Chosen by President Clinton to write and recite a poem for the presidential inauguration.

Further Reading

About Maya Angelou

Maya Angelou, by Miles Shapiro (Chelsea House, 1993).

About Black Authors and Poetry

Langston Hughes, American Poet, by Alice Walker (HarperCollins, 1974).

My Black Me: A Beginning Book of Black Poetry, edited by Arnold Adoff (Dutton, 1974).

Paul Laurence Dunbar: A Poet to Remember, by Patricia McKissack (Childrens Press, 1984).

Zora Neale Hurston, by Roz Colbert (Chelsea House, 1993).

Index